MW00491052

To Celebrate

_____

_____

Date

_____

THANK YOU FOR COMING.

Let's celebrate!

Guest Name

_____

Wishes & Messages

_____

_____

_____

_____

_____

EMAIL/PHONE

Guest Name

_____

Wishes & Messages

_____

_____

_____

_____

_____

_____

Email/Phone _____

Guest Name

_____

Wishes & Messages

_____

_____

_____

_____

_____

_____

_____

EMAIL/PHONE

Guest Name

Wishes & Messages

Email/Phone

Guest Name

_____

Wishes & Messages

_____

_____

_____

_____

_____

_____

EMAIL/PHONE

Guest Name

Wishes & Messages

EMAIL/PHONE

Guest Name

Wishes & Messages

EMAIL/PHONE

Guest Name

Wishes & Messages

EMAIL/PHONE

Guest Name

_____

Wishes & Messages

_____

_____

_____

_____

_____

_____

EMAIL/PHONE
_____

Guest Name

_____

Wishes & Messages

_____

_____

_____

_____

_____

_____

EMAIL/PHONE

Guest Name

_____

Wishes & Messages

_____

_____

_____

_____

_____

_____

EMAIL/PHONE _____

Guest Name

Wishes & Messages

EMAIL/PHONE

Guest Name

_____

Wishes & Messages

_____

_____

_____

_____

_____

_____

Email/Phone
_____

Guest Name

Wishes & Messages

E
M
EMAIL/PHONE

Guest Name

Wishes & Messages

EMAIL/PHONE

Guest Name

Wishes & Messages

EMAIL/PHONE

Guest Name

_____

Wishes & Messages

_____

_____

_____

_____

_____

_____

EMAIL/PHONE

Guest Name

Wishes & Messages

EMAIL/PHONE

Guest Name

Wishes & Messages

EMAIL/PHONE

Guest Name

_____

Wishes & Messages

_____

_____

_____

_____

_____

_____

EMAIL/PHONE _____

Guest Name

Wishes & Messages

EMAIL/PHONE

Guest Name

_____

Wishes & Messages

_____

_____

_____

_____

_____

_____

EMAIL/PHONE
_____

Guest Name

_____

Wishes & Messages

_____

_____

_____

_____

_____

Email/Phone

_____

Guest Name

Wishes & Messages

Email/Phone

Guest Name

_____

Wishes & Messages

_____

_____

_____

_____

_____

Email/Phone
_____

Guest Name

Wishes & Messages

EMAIL/PHONE

Guest Name

_____

Wishes & Messages

_____

_____

_____

_____

_____

EMAIL/PHONE

Guest Name

_____

Wishes & Messages

_____

_____

_____

_____

_____

_____

Email/Phone _____

Guest Name

_____

Wishes & Messages

_____

_____

_____

_____

_____

_____

EMAIL/PHONE
_____

Guest Name

Wishes & Messages

EMAIL/PHONE

Guest Name

Wishes & Messages

EMAIL/PHONE

Guest Name

Wishes & Messages

EMAIL/PHONE

Guest Name

Wishes & Messages

EMAIL/PHONE

Guest Name

Wishes & Messages

_____

_____

_____

_____

_____

_____

EMAIL/PHONE

Guest Name

_____

Wishes & Messages

_____

_____

_____

_____

_____

_____

EMAIL/PHONE

Guest Name

_____

Wishes & Messages

_____

_____

_____

_____

_____

Email/Phone _____

Guest Name

_____

Wishes & Messages

_____

_____

_____

_____

_____

_____

Email/Phone

Guest Name

Wishes & Messages

EMAIL/PHONE

Guest Name

Wishes & Messages

EMAIL/PHONE

Guest Name

Wishes & Messages

Email/Phone

Guest Name

Wishes & Messages

EMAIL/PHONE

Guest Name

_____

Wishes & Messages

_____

_____

_____

_____

_____

EMAIL/PHONE

Guest Name

Wishes & Messages

Email/Phone

Guest Name

Wishes & Messages

Email/Phone

Guest Name

Wishes & Messages

Email/Phone

Guest Name

Wishes & Messages

_____

_____

_____

_____

_____

_____

Email/Phone _____

Guest Name

_____

Wishes & Messages

_____

_____

_____

_____

_____

_____

EMAIL/PHONE
_____

Guest Name

Wishes & Messages

EMAIL/PHONE

Guest Name

_____

Wishes & Messages

_____

_____

_____

_____

_____

_____

Email/Phone
_____

Guest Name

Wishes & Messages

EMAIL/PHONE

Guest Name

_____

Wishes & Messages

_____

_____

_____

_____

_____

EMAIL/PHONE
_____

Guest Name

_____

Wishes & Messages

_____

_____

_____

_____

_____

_____

Email/Phone

Guest Name

_____

Wishes & Messages

_____

_____

_____

_____

_____

_____

EMAIL/PHONE
_____

Guest Name

Wishes & Messages

Email/Phone

Guest Name

Wishes & Messages

EMAIL/PHONE

Guest Name

Wishes & Messages

EMAIL/PHONE

Guest Name

Wishes & Messages

EMAIL/PHONE

Guest Name

_____

Wishes & Messages

_____

_____

_____

_____

_____

_____

Email/Phone
_____

Guest Name

Wishes & Messages

Email/Phone

Guest Name

Wishes & Messages

Email/Phone

Guest Name

_____

Wishes & Messages

_____

_____

_____

_____

_____

_____

EMAIL/PHONE

Guest Name

_____

Wishes & Messages

_____

_____

_____

_____

Email/Phone _____

Guest Name

_____

Wishes & Messages

_____

_____

_____

_____

_____

Email/Phone _____

Guest Name

_____

Wishes & Messages

_____

_____

_____

_____

_____

_____

Email/Phone _____

Guest Name

_____

Wishes & Messages

_____

_____

_____

_____

_____

_____

Email/Phone _____

Guest Name

Wishes & Messages

EMAIL/PHONE

Guest Name

_____

Wishes & Messages

_____

_____

_____

_____

_____

_____

EMAIL/PHONE
_____

Guest Name

_____

Wishes & Messages

_____

_____

_____

_____

_____

_____

EMAIL/PHONE

Guest Name

_____

Wishes & Messages

_____

_____

_____

_____

_____

_____

Email/Phone
_____

Guest Name

_____

Wishes & Messages

_____

_____

_____

_____

_____

_____

EMAIL/PHONE

Guest Name

Wishes & Messages

Email/Phone

Guest Name

Wishes & Messages

Email/Phone

Guest Name

Wishes & Messages

EMAIL/PHONE

Guest Name

Wishes & Messages

Email/Phone

Guest Name

Wishes & Messages

EMAIL/PHONE

Guest Name

_____

Wishes & Messages

_____

_____

_____

_____

_____

_____

EMAIL/PHONE

Guest Name

Wishes & Messages

Email/Phone

Guest Name

Wishes & Messages

_____

_____

_____

_____

_____

_____

Email/Phone

Guest Name

Wishes & Messages

E

EMAIL/PHONE

Guest Name

_____

Wishes & Messages

_____

_____

_____

_____

_____

_____

EMAIL/PHONE

Guest Name

_____

Wishes & Messages

_____

_____

_____

_____

_____

_____

EMAIL/PHONE _____

Guest Name

Wishes & Messages

Email/Phone

Guest Name

_____

Wishes & Messages

_____

_____

_____

_____

_____

_____

EMAIL/PHONE

Guest Name

_____

Wishes & Messages

_____

_____

_____

_____

_____

_____

EMAIL/PHONE _____

Guest Name

Wishes & Messages

_____

_____

_____

_____

_____

_____

EMAIL/PHONE

Guest Name

Wishes & Messages

Email/Phone

Guest Name

_____

Wishes & Messages

_____

_____

_____

_____

_____

_____

EMAIL/PHONE

Guest Name

Wishes & Messages

EMAIL/PHONE

Guest Name

_____

Wishes & Messages

_____

_____

_____

_____

_____

_____

Email/Phone
_____

Guest Name

_____

Wishes & Messages

_____

_____

_____

_____

_____

Email/Phone
_____

Guest Name

Wishes & Messages

Email/Phone

Guest Name

Wishes & Messages

EMAIL/PHONE

Guest Name

Wishes & Messages

EMAIL/PHONE

Guest Name

Wishes & Messages

EMAIL/PHONE

Guest Name

_____

Wishes & Messages

_____

_____

_____

_____

_____

_____

EMAIL/PHONE _____

Guest Name

Wishes & Messages

EMAIL/PHONE

Guest Name

Wishes & Messages

_____

_____

_____

_____

_____

_____

EMAIL/PHONE

Guest Name

_____

Wishes & Messages

_____

_____

_____

_____

_____

_____

EMAIL/PHONE

Guest Name

Wishes & Messages

Email/Phone

Guest Name

Wishes & Messages

EMAIL/PHONE

Guest Name

Wishes & Messages

EMAIL/PHONE

Guest Name

Wishes & Messages

EMAIL/PHONE

Guest Name

_____

Wishes & Messages

_____

_____

_____

_____

_____

_____

Email/Phone

NOTES & PHOTOS

GIFT LOG

Name / Email / Phone	Gift

GIFT LOG

Name / Email / Phone	Gift

GIFT LOG

Name / Email / Phone   *Gift*

_____   _____

_____   _____

_____   _____

_____   _____

_____   _____

_____   _____

_____   _____

_____   _____

_____   _____

_____   _____

_____   _____

_____   _____

GIFT LOG

Name / Email / Phone	Gift

GIFT LOG

Name / Email / Phone	Gift